The Emperor of Ice-Cream

and Other Poems

Wallace Stevens

DOVER PUBLICATIONS, INC.
Mineola, New York

Copyright

Copyright © 1999 by Dover Publications, Inc.
All rights reserved.

Bibliographical Note

This Dover edition, first published in 1999, and republished in 2005, is a new selection of 82 poems from standard texts. A new introductory Note was specially prepared for the 1999 edition. An alphabetical list of titles and an alphabetical list of first lines have been included in the present edition.

Library of Congress Cataloging-in-Publication Data

Stevens, Wallace, 1879–1955.
    The emperor of ice-cream, and other poems / Wallace Stevens.
    p. cm.
    ISBN-13: 978-0-486-44077-4 (pbk.)
    ISBN-10: 0-486-44077-X (pbk.)
    I. Title.

PS3537.T4753A6 2005
811'.52—dc22

2004059347

Manufactured in the United States by RR Donnelley
44077X03   2015
www.doverpublications.com

Note

WALLACE STEVENS was born in Reading, Pennsylvania, on
October 2, 1879. His father, raised as a farmer, became a
teacher, then a lawyer; Stevens's mother was a former teacher.
The second of five children, Stevens grew into a robust, bright
young man. He attended Harvard University from 1897 to 1900,
and helped edit the *Harvard Advocate,* where his verses and
stories appeared, his poetry catching the attention of an instruc-
tor, the philosopher George Santayana. Without graduating,
Stevens left for New York City, hoping to make his living writing
for newspapers. Two years of reporting and editing convinced
him of his lack of interest in journalism, and led him to enroll at
New York Law School. His deepest pleasure, however, was in
taking long, steady walks. On days off he regularly took strolls of
twenty-five to forty miles throughout the city, over bridges,
across rivers, and sometimes into the countryside and towns of
New Jersey. These intense, observant walks, recorded in his
journals, provided contemplative details and settings for his
poems years later.

His law career got off to a faltering start as he wandered from
one firm to another; he considered returning to Reading to work
for his father, as one of his brothers had done. Though he kept
journals and composed descriptive letters, he seems to have
written little poetry after leaving Harvard until he met the
woman who would become his wife, Elsie Kachel, in 1907, on
one of his visits home. She inspired him to write and collect
poems as gifts to her in two volumes, "A Book of Verses" and
"The Little June Book." Several verses from the second one sub-
sequently found publication in periodicals. His engagement to
Elsie provoked a complete split between himself and his family,
his father being strenuous in his objections to Stevens's choice.
Elsie was young and beautiful, but from the wrong side of the

tracks in class-conscious Reading. (Ironically, Stevens himself
would fume over his daughter's choice of a working-class
spouse.) In 1908, Stevens began legal work for an insurance
company and found his specialty in bonds. He and Elsie mar-
ried in 1909, but New York City, whose bustle and culture so
invigorated him, held little attraction for her.

In 1914, at the relatively late age of thirty-five, Stevens made
his deliberate entry onto the literary scene. His reputation as a
poet of dazzling language and intellectual badinage got off the
ground with "Carnet de Voyage," a series of poems published in
The Trend. Poems by this unknown insurance executive
appeared, in short order, in avant-garde magazines such as
Others, The Little Review, Rogue, and *Poetry*. These poems
would become some of the most famous in American literature,
including "Thirteen Ways of Looking at a Blackbird,"
"Peter Quince at the Clavier," and "Sunday Morning." (The
cropped, rearranged version of "Sunday Morning," edited by
Poetry's Harriet Monroe, is included in this volume.) In 1916,
an insurance company Stevens had joined in 1914 collapsed
financially. With many misgivings about abandoning his beloved
New York City, where he was suddenly involved in the bur-
geoning art scene, Stevens took a long-standing offer from a
friend in Connecticut to accept a post in a branch of the
Hartford Accident and Indemnity Company. He remained with
this firm to his death almost forty years later. Contrary to popu-
lar myth, Stevens, as private as he was about his writing and
home life, was certainly known by his coworkers and acquain-
tances in Hartford to be a poet of renown. But many of his
friends, associates, and family members were more baffled by
the peculiar linguistic twists and philosophical flashes of his
poetry than by Einstein's theory of relativity.

Meanwhile, a steadily growing audience of readers and edi-
tors found itself dazzled and delighted. In spite of the almost
immediate recognition and prizewinning success of his poems in
the late 1910s, Stevens showed little inclination to publish a
book, preferring, he said, the poems' scattershot appearance in
periodicals and anthologies. When *Harmonium* (most of whose
poems are presented in this volume) came out in 1923, there

was no great contemporary acclaim. His only child, Holly, who would after his death collect and publish his journals and letters, was born in 1924.

Stevens added fourteen poems to a new edition in 1931 of *Harmonium*, the publication of which began his ever-increasing popularity. He shunned publicity, but his poems became lightning rods of fascination and admiration to each new generation of students, professors, and writers. *Ideas of Order* was published by a small, fine press in 1935, and then reissued by Alfred A. Knopf in 1936. *Owl's Clover* (1936) and *The Man with the Blue Guitar* (1937) followed shortly. Despite his new fame, Stevens's job at the Hartford remained vitally important to him. His divided career as businessman and poet never seemed ill-fitting to him. At the Hartford, Stevens was characteristically astute, effective, and peculiarly forthright and independent. He was a leading authority on surety bond law and became one of three vice presidents at the company in 1934.

Though he avidly collected French and Asian books and paintings, he did not ever go abroad. He travelled on business through the U.S. and spent many winters vacationing in Florida, an occasional backdrop for his poems. Portly, austere-seeming, and conservative-minded, he never learned to drive, and he could be seen in Hartford on his daily walks to and from his affluent neighborhood. He was protective of this slow-paced activity, because he used it to muse over his writing and whet his insatiable appetite for fine and evocative words. Though he declined most invitations, he read to public gatherings in New York City and at college campuses from the late 1930s into the 1950s. Before the end of his life he published several more volumes: *Parts of a World* (1942), *Notes toward a Supreme Fiction* (1942), *Esthétique du Mal* (1945), *Transport to Summer* (1947), *Auroras of Autumn* (1950), *The Necessary Angel: Essays on Reality and the Imagination* (1951), which was his only book of prose, and, finally, *The Collected Poems* in 1954, for which he received the National Book Award. In 1955, not long after receiving the Pulitzer Prize in May, Stevens died on August 2.

The poems in this volume include all of those published in magazines, journals, and anthologies from 1914 through 1922.

For her advice and criticism, I thank Kia Penso, author of *Wallace Stevens, Harmonium, and the Whole of Harmonium* (Archon, 1991). For their help in making copies of rare periodicals accessible, I thank the librarians of Columbia University, McMaster University, the New York Public Library, and the NYPL's Berg Collection.

BOB BLAISDELL

Contents

	page
Carnet de Voyage	1
From a Junk	4
Home Again	4
Phases	4
Tea	6
Cy Est Pourtraicte, Madame Ste Ursule, et Les Unze Mille Vierges	6
Peter Quince at the Clavier	7
The Silver Plough-Boy	10
Disillusionment of Ten O'Clock	10
Sunday Morning	11
Domination of Black	13
Tattoo	14
The Florist Wears Knee-Breeches	15
Song	15
Six Significant Landscapes	16
Inscription for a Monument	18
Bowl	18
The Worms at Heaven's Gate	19
Primordia	19
To the Roaring Wind	22
Valley Candle	22
Thirteen Ways of Looking at a Blackbird	23
The Wind Shifts	25
Meditation	26
Gray Room	26

page

Explanation	27
Theory	27
The Plot Against the Giant	28
"Lettres d'un Soldat"	29
Anecdote of Men by the Thousand	35
Metaphors of a Magnifico	36
Depression Before Spring	37
Earthy Anecdote	37
Moment of Light	38
Le Monocle de Mon Oncle	40
Architecture for the Adoration of Beauty	44
Nuances of a Theme by Williams	47
Anecdote of Canna	47
The Apostrophe to Vincentine	48
Life Is Motion	49
Fabliau of Florida	49
Homunculus et La Belle Etoile	50
The Weeping Burgher	51
Peter Parasol	52
Exposition of the Contents of a Cab	53
Ploughing on Sunday	53
Banal Sojourn	54
The Indigo Glass in the Grass	55
Anecdote of the Jar	55
Of the Surface of Things	55
The Curtains in the House of the Metaphysician	56
The Place of the Solitaires	56
The Paltry Nude Starts on a Spring Voyage	57
Colloquy with a Polish Aunt	58
Invective Against Swans	58
Infanta Marina	59
Cortège for Rosenbloom	60
The Man Whose Pharynx Was Bad	61
Palace of the Babies	62

page

From the Misery of Don Joost	63
The Doctor of Geneva	63
Gubbinal	64
The Snow Man	64
Tea at the Palaz of Hoon	65
The Cuban Doctor	66
Another Weeping Woman	66
Of the Manner of Addressing Clouds	67
Of Heaven Considered as a Tomb	67
The Load of Sugar-Cane	68
Hibiscus on the Sleeping Shores	68
The Bird with the Coppery, Keen Claws	69
Lulu Gay	70
Lulu Morose	70
Hymn from a Watermelon Pavilion	71
Stars at Tallapoosa	72
Bantams in Pine-Woods	72
The Ordinary Women	73
Frogs Eat Butterflies. Snakes Eat Frogs. Hogs Eat Snakes. Men Eat Hogs	74
A High-Toned Old Christian Woman	75
O, Florida, Venereal Soil	76
The Emperor of Ice-Cream	77
To the One of Fictive Music	77
Alphabetical List of Titles	79
Alphabetical List of First Lines	82

Carnet de Voyage

I

An odor from a star
Comes to my fancy, slight,
Tenderly spiced and gay,
As if a seraph's hand
Unloosed the fragrant silks
Of some sultana, bright
In her soft sky. And pure
It is, and excellent,
As if a seraph's blue
Fell, as a shadow falls,
And his warm body shed
Sweet exhalations, void
Of our despised decay.

II

One More Sunset

The green goes from the corn,
The blue from all the lakes,
And the shadows of the mountains mingle in the sky.

Far off, the still bamboo
Grows green; the desert pool
Turns gaudy turquoise for the chanting caravan.

The changing green and blue
Flow round the changing earth;
And all the rest is empty wondering and sleep.

III

Here the grass grows,
And the wind blows.
And in the stream,
Small fishes gleam,
Blood-red and hue
Of shadowy blue,
And amber sheen,
And water-green,
And yellow flash,
And diamond ash.
And the grass grows,
And the wind blows.

IV

She that winked her sandal fan
Long ago in gray Japan—

She that heard the bell intone
Rendezvous by rolling Rhone—

How wide the spectacle of sleep,
Hands folded, eyes too still to weep!

V

I am weary of the plum and of the cherry,
And that buff moon in evening's aquarelle,
I have no heart within to make me merry.
I nod above the books of Heaven or Hell.

All things are old. The new-born swallows fare
Through the Spring twilight on dead September's wing.
The dust of Babylon is in the air,
And settles on my lips the while I sing.

VI

Man from the waste evolved
The Cytherean glade,
Imposed on battering seas
His keel's dividing blade,
And sailed there, unafraid.

The isle revealed his worth.
It was a place to sing in
And honor noble Life,
For white doves to wing in,
And roses to spring in.

VII

Chinese Rocket

There, a rocket in the Wain
Brings primeval night again.
All the startled heavens flare
From the Shepherd to the Bear—

When the old-time dark returns,
Lo, the steadfast lady burns
Her curious lantern to disclose
How calmly the White River flows!

VIII

On an Old Guitar

It was a simple thing
For her to sit and sing,
    "Hey nonino!"

This year and that befell,
(Time saw and Time can tell),
    With a hey and a ho—

Under the peach-tree, play
Such mockery away,
    Hey nonino!

From a Junk

A great fish plunges in the dark,
Its fins of rutted silver; sides,
Belabored with a foamy light;
And back, brilliant with scaly salt.
It glistens in the flapping wind,
Burns there and glistens, wide and wide,
Under the five-horned stars of night,
In wind and wave . . . It is the moon.

Home Again

Back within the valley,
Down from the divide,
No more flaming clouds about,
O! the soft hillside,
And my cottage light,
And the starry night.

Phases

I

There's a little square in Paris,
Waiting until we pass.
They sit idly there,
They sip the glass.

There's a cab-horse at the corner,
There's rain. The season grieves.
It was silver once,
And green with leaves.

There's a parrot in a window,
Will see us on parade,
Hear the loud drums roll—
And serenade.

II

This was the salty taste of glory,
That it was not
Like Agamemnon's story.
Only, an eyeball in the mud,
And Hopkins,
Flat and pale and gory!

III

But the bugles, in the night,
Were wings that bore
To where our comfort was;

Arabesques of candle beams,
Winding
Through our heavy dreams;

Winds that blew
Where the bending iris grew;

Birds of intermitted bliss,
Singing in the night's abyss;

Vines with yellow fruit,
That fell
Along the walls
That bordered Hell.

IV

Death's nobility again
Beautified the simplest men.
Fallen Winkle felt the pride
Of Agamemnon
When he died.

What could London's
Work and waste
Give him—
To that salty, sacrificial taste?

What could London's
Sorrow bring—
To that short, triumphant sting?

Tea

When the elephant's-ear in the park
Shrivelled in frost,
And the leaves on the paths
Ran like rats,
Your lamp-light fell
On shining pillows,
Of sea-shades and sky-shades,
Like umbrellas in Java.

Cy Est Pourtraicte, Madame Ste Ursule, et Les Unze Mille Vierges

Ursula, in a garden, found
A bed of radishes.
She kneeled upon the ground
And gathered them,
With flowers around,
Blue, gold, pink and green.

She dressed in red and gold brocade
And in the grass an offering made
Of radishes and flowers.

She said, "My dear,
Upon your altars,
I have placed
The marguerite and coquelicot,
And roses
Frail as April snow;
But here"; she said,
"Where none can see,
I make an offering, in the grass,
Of radishes and flowers."
And then she wept
For fear the Lord would not accept.

The good Lord in His garden sought
New leaf and shadowy tinct,
And they were all His thought.
He heard her low accord,
Half prayer and half ditty,
And He felt a subtle quiver,
That was not heavenly love,
Or pity.

This is not writ
In any book.

Peter Quince at the Clavier

I

Just as my fingers on these keys
Make music, so the self-same sounds
On my spirit make a music, too.

Music is feeling, then, not sound;
And thus it is that what I feel,
Here in this room, desiring you,

Thinking of your blue-shadowed silk,
Is music. It is like the strain
Waked in the elders by Susanna:

Of a green evening, clear and warm,
She bathed in her still garden, while
The red-eyed elders, watching, felt

The basses of their beings throb
In witching chords, and their thin blood
Pulse pizzicati of Hosanna.

II

In the green water, clear and warm,
Susanna lay.
She searched
The touch of springs,
And found
Concealed imaginings.
She sighed,
For so much melody.

Upon the bank, she stood
In the cool
Of spent emotions.
She felt, among the leaves,
The dew
Of old devotions.

She walked upon the grass,
Still quavering.
The winds were like her maids,

On timid feet,
Fetching her woven scarves,
Yet wavering.

A breath upon her hand
Muted the night.
She turned—
A cymbal crashed,
And roaring horns.

III

Soon, with a noise like tambourines,
Came her attendant Byzantines.

They wondered why Susanna cried
Against the elders by her side;

And as they whispered, the refrain
Was like a willow swept by rain.

Anon, their lamps' uplifted flame
Revealed Susanna and her shame.

And then, the simpering Byzantines,
Fled, with a noise like tambourines.

IV

Beauty is momentary in the mind—
The fitful tracing of a portal;
But in the flesh it is immortal.

The body dies; the body's beauty lives.
So evenings die, in their green going,
A wave, interminably flowing.
So gardens die, their meek breath scenting

The cowl of Winter, done repenting.
So maidens die, to the auroral
Celebration of a maiden's choral.

Susanna's music touched the bawdy strings
Of those white elders; but, escaping,
Left only Death's ironic scraping.
Now, in its immortality, it plays
On the clear viol of her memory,
And makes a constant sacrament of praise.

The Silver Plough-Boy

A black figure dances in a black field.
It seizes a sheet—from the ground, from a bush—as if spread
      there by some wash-woman for the night.
It wraps the sheet around its body, until the black figure is silver.
It dances down a furrow, in the early light, back of a crazy
      plough, the green blades following.
How soon the silver fades in the dust! How soon the black
      figure slips from the wrinkled sheet! How softly the
      sheet falls to the ground!

Disillusionment of Ten O'Clock

The houses are haunted
By white night-gowns.
None are green,
Or purple with green rings,
Or green with yellow rings,
Or yellow with blue rings,
None of them are strange,
With socks of lace
And beaded ceintures.

People are not going
To dream of baboons and periwinkles.
Only, here and there, an old sailor,
Drunk and asleep in his boots,
Catches tigers
In red weather.

Sunday Morning

I

Complacencies of the peignoir, and late
Coffee and oranges in a sunny chair,
And the green freedom of a cockatoo
Upon a rug, mingle to dissipate
The holy hush of ancient sacrifice.
She dreams a little, and she feels the dark
Encroachment of that old catastrophe,
As a calm darkens among water-lights.
The pungent oranges and bright, green wings
Seem things in some procession of the dead,
Winding across wide water, without sound.
The day is like wide water, without sound,
Stilled for the passing of her dreaming feet
Over the seas, to silent Palestine,
Dominion of the blood and sepulcher.

II

She hears, upon that water without sound,
A voice that cries, "The tomb in Palestine
Is not the porch of spirits lingering;
It is the grave of Jesus, where he lay."
We live in an old chaos of the sun,
Or old dependency of day and night,
Or island solitude, unsponsored, free,
Of that wide water, inescapable.

Deer walk upon our mountains, and the quail
Whistle about us their spontaneous cries;
Sweet berries ripen in the wilderness;
And, in the isolation of the sky,
At evening, casual flocks of pigeons make
Ambiguous undulations as they sink,
Downward to darkness, on extended wings.

III

She says, "I am content when wakened birds,
Before they fly, test the reality
Of misty fields, by their sweet questionings;
But when the birds are gone, and their warm fields
Return no more, where, then, is paradise?"
There is not any haunt of prophecy,
Nor any old chimera of the grave,
Neither the golden underground, nor isle
Melodious, where spirits gat them home,
Nor visionary South, nor cloudy palm
Remote on heaven's hill, that has endured
As April's green endures; or will endure
Like her remembrance of awakened birds,
Or her desire for June and evening, tipped
By the consummation of the swallow's wings.

IV

She says, "But in contentment I still feel
The need of some imperishable bliss."
Death is the mother of beauty; hence from her,
Alone, shall come fulfilment to our dreams
And our desires. Although she strews the leaves
Of sure obliteration on our paths—
The path sick sorrow took, the many paths
Where triumph rang its brassy phrase, or love
Whispered a little out of tenderness—
She makes the willow shiver in the sun

For maidens who were wont to sit and gaze
Upon the grass, relinquished to their feet.
She causes boys to bring sweet-smelling pears
And plums in ponderous piles. The maidens taste
And stray impassioned in the littering leaves.

V

Supple and turbulent, a ring of men
Shall chant in orgy on a summer morn
Their boisterous devotion to the sun—
Not as a god, but as a god might be,
Naked among them, like a savage source.
Their chant shall be a chant of paradise,
Out of their blood, returning to the sky;
And in their chant shall enter, voice by voice,
The windy lake wherein their lord delights,
The trees, like seraphim, and echoing hills,
That choir among themselves long afterward.
They shall know well the heavenly fellowship
Of men that perish and of summer morn—
And whence they came and whither they shall go,
The dew upon their feet shall manifest.

Domination of Black

At night, by the fire,
The colors of the bushes
And of the fallen leaves,
Repeating themselves,
Turned in the room,
Like the leaves themselves
Turning in the wind.
Yes: but the color of the heavy hemlocks
Came striding—
And I remembered the cry of the peacocks

The colors of their tails
Were like the leaves themselves
Turning in the wind,
In the twilight wind.
They swept over the room,
Just as they flew from the boughs of the hemlocks
Down to the ground.
I heard them cry—the peacocks.
Was it a cry against the twilight
Or against the leaves themselves
Turning in the wind,
Turning as the flames
Turned in the fire,
Turning as the tails of the peacocks
Turned in the loud fire,
Loud as the hemlocks
Full of the cry of the peacocks?
Or was it a cry against the hemlocks?

Out of the window,
I saw how the planets gathered
Like the leaves themselves
Turning in the wind.
I saw how the night came,
Came striding like the color of the heavy hemlocks.
I felt afraid—
And I remembered the cry of the peacocks.

Tattoo

The light is like a spider.
It crawls over the water.
It crawls over the edges of the snow.
It crawls under your eyelids
And spreads its webs there—
Its two webs.

The webs of your eyes
Are fastened
To the flesh and bones of you
As to rafters or grass.

There are filaments of your eyes
On the surface of the water
And in the edges of the snow.

The Florist Wears Knee-Breeches

My flowers are reflected
In your mind
As you are reflected in your glass.
When you look at them,
There is nothing in your mind
Except the reflections
Of my flowers.
But when I look at them
I see only the reflections
In your mind,
And not my flowers.
It is my desire
To bring roses,
And place them before you
In a white dish.

Song

There are great things doing
In the world,
Little rabbit.
There is a damsel,
Sweeter than the sound of the willow,

Dearer than shallow water
Flowing over pebbles.
Of a Sunday,
She wears a long coat,
With twelve buttons on it.
Tell that to your mother.

Six Significant Landscapes

I

An old man sits
In the shadow of a pine tree
In China.
He sees larkspur,
Blue and white,
At the edge of the shadow,
Move in the wind.
His beard moves in the wind.
The pine tree moves in the wind.
Thus water flows
Over weeds.

II

The night is of the color
Of a woman's arm:
Night, the female,
Obscure,
Fragrant and supple,
Conceals herself,
A pool shines,
Like a bracelet
Shaken in a dance.

III

I measure myself
Against a tall tree.
I find that I am much taller,
For I reach right up to the sun,
With my eye;
And I reach to the shore of the sea
With my ear.
Nevertheless, I dislike
The way the ants crawl
In and out of my shadow.

IV

When my dream was near the moon,
The white folds of its gown
Filled with yellow light.
The soles of its feet
Grew red.
Its hair filled
With certain blue crystallizations
From stars,
Not far off.

V

Not all the knives of the lamp-posts,
Nor the chisels of the long streets,
Nor the mallets of the domes
And high towers,
Can carve
What one star can carve,
Shining through the grape-leaves.

VI

Rationalists, wearing square hats,
Think, in square rooms,
Looking at the floor,
Looking at the ceiling.
They confine themselves
To right-angled triangles.
If they tried rhomboids,
Cones, waving lines, ellipses—
As, for example, the ellipse of the half-moon—
Rationalists would wear sombreros.

Inscription for a Monument

To the imagined lives
Evoked by music,
Creatures of horns, flutes, drums,
Violins, bassoons, cymbals—
Nude porters that glistened in Burma
Defiling from sight;
Island philosophers spent
By long thought beside fountains;
Big-bellied ogres curled up in the sunlight,
Stuttering dreams. . . .

Bowl

For what emperor
Was this bowl of Earth designed?
Here are more things
Than on any bowl of the Sungs,
Even the rarest—
Vines that take
The various obscurities of the moon,
Approaching rain

And leaves that would be loose upon the wind,
Pears on pointed trees,
The dresses of women,
Oxen . . .
I never tire
To think of this.

The Worms at Heaven's Gate

Out of the tomb, we bring Badroulbadour,
Within our bellies, we her chariot,
Here is an eye. And here are, one by one,
The lashes of that eye and its white lid.
Here is the cheek on which that lid declined,
And, finger after finger, here, the hand,
The genius of that cheek. Here are the lips,
The bundle of the body and the feet.

                    .   .   .   .   .   .

Out of the tomb we bring Badroulbadour.

Primordia

In the Northwest

1

All over Minnesota,
Cerise sopranos,
Walking in the snow,
Answer, humming,
The male voice of the wind in the dry leaves
Of the lake-hollows.
For one,
The syllables of the gulls and of the crows
And of the blue-bird
Meet in the name

Of Jalmar Lillygreen.
There is his motion
In the flowing of black water.

2

The child's hair is of the color of the hay in the haystack, around
    which the four black horses stand.
There is the same color in the bellies of frogs, in clays, withered
    reeds, skins, wood, sunlight.

3

The blunt ice flows down the Mississippi,
At night.
In the morning, the clear river
Is full of reflections,
Beautiful alliterations of shadows and of things shadowed.

4

The horses gnaw the bark from the trees.
The horses are hollow,
The trunks of the trees are hollow.
Why do the horses have eyes and ears?
The trees do not.
Why can the horses move about on the ground?
The trees cannot.
The horses weary themselves hunting for green grass.
The trees stand still,
The trees drink.
The water runs away from the horses.
La, la, la, la, la, la, la, la.
Dee, dum, diddle, dee, dee, diddle, dee, da.

5

The birch trees draw up whiteness from the ground.
In the swamps, bushes draw up dark red,
Or yellow.

O, boatman,
What are you drawing from the rain-pointed water?
O, boatman,
What are you drawing from the rain-pointed water?
Are you two boatmen
Different from each other?

In the South

6

Unctuous furrows,
The ploughman portrays in you
The spring about him:
Compilation of the effects
Of magenta blooming in the Judas-tree
And of purple blooming in the eucalyptus—
Map of yesterday's earth
And of to-morrow's heaven.

7

The lilacs wither in the Carolinas.
Already the butterflies flutter above the cabins.
Already the new-born children interpret love
In the voices of mothers.
Timeless mother,
How is it that your aspic nipples
For once vent honey?

The pine-tree sweetens my body.
The white iris beautifies me.

8

The black mother of eleven children
Hangs her quilt under the pine-trees.
There is a connection between the colors,
The shapes of the patches,
And the eleven children . . .

Frail princes of distant Monaco,
That paragon of a parasol
Discloses
At least one baby in you.

9

The trade-wind jingles the rings in the nets around the racks by
the docks on Indian River.
It is the same jingle of the water among the roots under the
banks of the palmettoes,
It is the same jingle of the red-bird breasting the orange-trees
out of the cedars.
Yet there is no spring in Florida, neither in boskage perdu, nor
on the nunnery beaches.

To the Roaring Wind

What syllable are you seeking,
Vocalissimus,
In the distances of sleep?
Speak it.

Valley Candle

My candle burned alone in an immense valley.
Beams of the huge night converged upon it,
Until the wind blew.
Then beams of the huge night
Converged upon its image,
Until the wind blew.

Thirteen Ways of Looking at a Blackbird

I

Among twenty snowy mountains,
The only moving thing
Was the eye of the blackbird.

II

I was of three minds,
Like a tree
In which there are three blackbirds.

III

The blackbird whirled in the autumn winds,
It was a small part of the pantomime.

IV

A man and a woman
Are one.
A man and a woman and a blackbird
Are one.

V

I do not know which to prefer—
The beauty of inflections
Or the beauty of innuendoes,
The blackbird whistling
Or just after.

VI

Icicles filled the long window
With barbaric glass.
The shadow of the blackbird

Crossed it, to and fro.
The mood
Traced in the shadow
An indecipherable cause.

VII

O thin men of Haddam,
Why do you imagine golden birds?
Do you not see how the blackbird
Walks around the feet
Of the women about you?

VIII

I know noble accents
And lucid, inescapable rhythms;
But I know, too,
That the blackbird is involved
In what I know.

IX

When the blackbird flew out of sight,
It marked the edge
Of one of many circles.

X

At the sight of blackbirds
Flying in a green light,
Even the bawds of euphony
Would cry out sharply.

XI

He rode over Connecticut
In a glass coach.
Once, a fear pierced him,

In that he mistook
The shadow of his equipage
For blackbirds.

XII

The river is moving.
The blackbird must be flying.

XIII

It was evening all afternoon.
It was snowing
And it was going to snow.
The blackbird sat
In the cedar-limbs.

The Wind Shifts

This is how the wind shifts:
Like the thoughts of an old human,
Who still thinks eagerly
And despairingly.
The wind shifts like this:
Like a human without illusions,
Who still feels irrational things within her.
The wind shifts like this:
Like humans approaching proudly,
Like humans approaching angrily.
This is how the wind shifts:
Like a human, heavy and heavy,
Who does not care.

Meditation

How long have I meditated, O Prince,
On sky and earth?
It comes to this,
That even the moon
Has exhausted its emotions.
What is it that I think of, truly?
The lines of blackberry bushes,
The design of leaves—
Neither sky nor earth
Express themselves before me . . .
Bossuet did not preach at the funerals
Of puppets.

Gray Room

Although you sit in a room that is gray,
Except for the silver
Of the straw-paper,
And pick
At your pale white gown;
Or lift one of the green beads
Of your necklace,
To let it fall;
Or gaze at your green fan
Printed with the red branches of a red willow;
Or, with one finger,
Move the leaf in the bowl—
The leaf that has fallen from the branches of the
        forsythia
Beside you . . .
What is all this?
I know how furiously your heart is beating.

Explanation

Ach, Mutter,
This old, black dress—
I have been embroidering
French flowers on it.

Not by way of romance—
Here is nothing of the ideal,
Nein,
Nein.

It would have been different,
Liebchen,
If I had imagined myself,
In an orange gown,
Drifting through space,
Like a figure on the church-wall.

Theory

I am what is around me.

Women understand this.
One is not duchess
A hundred yards from a carriage.

These, then, are portraits:
A black vestibule leading to a wrought-iron grille;
A high bed sheltered by a canopy and curtains;
A row of amber statuettes.

These are merely instances.

The Plot Against the Giant

First Girl

When this yokel comes maundering
Whetting his hacker,
I shall run before him,
Diffusing the civilest odors
Out of geraniums and unsmelled flowers.
It will check him.

Second Girl

I shall run before him,
Arching cloths besprinkled with colors
As small as fish-eggs.
The threads
Will abash him.

Third Girl

Oh, la . . . le pauvre!
I shall run before him,
With a curious puffing,
He will bend his ear then.
I shall whisper
Heavenly labials in a world of gutturals.
It will undo him.

"Lettres d'un Soldat"

Combattre avec sés frères, à sa place, à son rang, avec des yeux dessillés, sans espoir de la gloire et de profit, et simplement parceque telle est la loi, voilà le commandement que donne le dieu au guerrier Arjuna, quand celui-ci doute s'il doit se détourner de l'absolu pour le cauchemar humain de la bataille. . . . Simplement qu'Arjuna bande son arc avec les autres Kshettryas![1] (Préface d'André Chevrillon.)

I

Jamais la majesté de la nuit ne m'apporta autant de consolation qu'en cette accumulation d'épreuves. Vénus, étincelante, m'est une amie.[2]   (27 septembre)

> The spirit wakes in the night wind—is naked.
> What is it that hides in the night wind
> Near by it?
>
> Is it, once more, the mysterious beauté,
> Like a woman inhibiting passion
> In solace?—
>
> The multiform beauty, sinking in night wind,
> Quick to be gone, yet never
> Quite going!

---

[1] "To fight with his brothers, in his place, in his rank, with his eyes open wide, without hope of glory or profit, and simply because this is the law, here is the commandment that God gives the warrior Arjuna, when he doubts if he ought to turn away from the absolute toward the human nightmare of battle. . . . Simply, allow Arjuna to bend his bow with the other Kshettryas!"

Stevens chose the following epigraphs from *Lettres d'un soldat* (1916), a book of letters sent home from the western front by a French soldier named Eugène Emmanuel Lemercier.

[2] "The majesty of night never brought me as much consolation as this set of trials. Dazzling Venus is my friend."

> She will leap back from the swift constellations,
> As they enter the place of their western
> Seclusion.

II

Ce qu'il faut, c'est reconnaître l'amour et la beauté triom-
phante de toute violence.[3]   *(22 octobre)*

Anecdotal Revery

The streets contain a crowd
Of blind men tapping their way
By inches—
This man to complain to the grocer
Of yesterday's cheese,
This man to visit a woman,
This man to take the air.
Am I to pick my way
Through these crickets?—
I, that have a head
In the bag
Slung over my shoulder!
I have secrets
That prick
Like a heart full of pins.
Permit me, gentlemen,
I have killed the mayor
And am escaping from you.
Get out of the way!
      (The blind men strike him down with their sticks.)

---

[3] "What has to be done is recognize the love and triumphant beauty of all
violence."

III

*Jusqu'à présent j'ai possédé une sagesse de renoncement, mais
maintenant je veux une sagesse qui accepte tout, en s'orientant
vers l'action future.*[4]   (*31 octobre*)

Morale

And so France feels. A menace that impends,
Too long, is like a bayonet that bends.

IV

*Si tu voyais la sécurité des petits animaux des bois—souris,
mulots! L'autre jour, dans notre abri de feuillage, je suivais les
évolutions de ces petits bêtes. Elles étaient jolies comme une
estampe japonaise, avec l'intérieur de leurs oreilles rose comme
un coquillage.*[5]   (*7 novembre*)

Comme Dieu Dispense de Graces

Here I keep thinking of the Primitives—
The sensitive and conscientious schemes
Of mountain pallors ebbing into air;

And I remember sharp Japonica—
The driving rain, the willows in the rain,
The birds that wait out rain in willow trees.

Although life seems a goblin mummery,
These images return and are increased,
As for a child in an oblivion:

---

[4] "Until now, I have possessed a wisdom of renunciation, but now I need a wisdom which accepts everything, and prepares for future action."

[5] "If you saw the sense of security of the little woodland animals—mice, field mice! The other day, in our leafy shelter, I observed the movements of these little creatures. They were as beautiful as a Japanese print, the inside of their ears pink as shells."

Even by mice—these scamper and are still.
They cock small ears, more glistening and pale
Than fragile volutes in a rose sea-shell.

V

*J'ai la ferme espérance; mais surtout j'ai confiance en la jus-
tice éternelle, quelque surprise qu'elle cause à l'humaine idée
que nous en avons.*[6]   *(26 novembre)*

The Surprises of the Superhuman

The palais de justice of chambermaids
Tops the horizon with its colonnades.

If it were lost in Uebermenschlichkeit,
Perhaps our wretched state would soon come right.

For somehow the brave dicta of its kings
Make more awry our faulty human things.

VI

*Bien chère mère aimée, . . . Pour ce qui est de ton cœur, j'ai
tellement confiance en ton courage, qu'à l'heure actuelle cette
certitude est mon grand réconfort. Je sais que ma mère a atteint
à cette liberté d'âme qui permet de contempler le spectacle
universel.*[7]   *(7 décembre)*

There is another mother whom I love,
O chère maman, another, who, in turn,
Is mother to the two of us, and more,

---

[6] "I have firm hope; but particularly I have confidence in eternal justice, how-
ever much it might surprise our idea of it."

[7] "My good dear mother, . . . As for what is in your heart, I am so sure of your
courage, that right now this certainty is my great comfort. I know my mother
achieved this freedom of the soul that permits her to contemplate the
universal spectacle."

In whose hard service both of us endure
Our petty portion in the sacrifice.
Not France! France also serves the invincible eye,
That, from her helmet terrible and bright,
Commands the armies; the relentless arm,
Devising proud, majestic issuance.
Wait now; have no rememberings of hope,
Poor penury. There will be voluble hymns
Come swelling, when, regardless of my end,
The mightier mother raises up her cry:
And little will or wish, that day, for tears.

VII

La seule sanction pour moi est ma conscience. Il faut nous confier à une justice impersonelle, indépendante de tout facteur humain; et à une destinée utile et harmonieuse malgré toute horreur de forme.[8]   *(15 janvier)*

Negation

Hi! The creator too is blind,
Struggling toward his harmonious whole,
Rejecting intermediate parts—
Horrors and falsities and wrongs;
Incapable master of all force,
Too vague idealist, overwhelmed
By an afflatus that persists.
For this, then, we endure brief lives,
The evanescent symmetries
From that meticulous potter's thumb.

---

[8] "The only safeguard for me is my conscience. It is necessary for us to trust in an impersonal justice, independent of any human factor; and in a useful, harmonious destiny despite its horrible form."

VIII

Hier soir, rentrant dans ma grange, ivresse, rixes, cris, chants,
et hurlements. Voilà la vie![9]   *(4 février)*

John Smith and his son John Smith,
  And his son's son John, and-a-one
  And-a-two and-a-three
And-a-rum-tum-tum, and-a
Lean John, and his son, lean John,
  And his lean son's John, and-a-one
  And-a-two and-a-three
And-a-drum-rum-rum, and-a
Rich John, and his son, rich John,
  And his rich son's John, and-a-one
  And-a-two and-a-three
And-a-pom-pom-pom, and-a
Wise John, and his son, wise John,
  And his wise son's John, and-a-one
  And-a-two and-a-three
  And-a-fee and-a-fee and-a-fee
  And-a-fee-fo-fum—
  Voilà la vie, la vie, la vie,
  And-a-rummy-tummy-tum
  And-a-rummy-tummy-tum.

IX

La mort du soldat est près des choses naturelles.[10]   *(5 mars)*

Life contracts and death is expected,
As in a season of autumn.
The soldier falls.

---

[9] "Last night, returning to my barn, ecstacy, cries, shouts, and roars. Such is life!"
[10] "The death of a soldier is almost a natural thing."

He does not become a three-days' personage,
Imposing his separation,
Calling for pomp.

Death is absolute and without memorial,
As in a season of autumn,
When the wind stops.

When the wind stops and, over the heavens,
The clouds go, nevertheless,
In their direction.

Anecdote of Men by the Thousand

The soul, he said, is composed
Of the external world.

There are men of the East, he said,
Who are the East.
There are men of a province
Who are that province.
There are men of a valley
Who are that valley.

There are men whose words
Are as natural sounds
Of their places
As the cackle of toucans
In the place of toucans.

The mandoline is the instrument
Of a place.

Are there mandolines of Western mountains?
Are there mandolines of Northern moonlight?

The dress of a woman of Lhassa,
In its place,
Is an invisible element of that place
Made visible.

Metaphors of a Magnifico

Twenty men crossing a bridge,
Into a village,
Are twenty men crossing twenty bridges,
Into twenty villages,
Or one man
Crossing a single bridge into a village.

This is old song
That will not declare itself . . .

Twenty men crossing a bridge,
Into a village,
Are
Twenty men crossing a bridge
Into a village.

That will not declare itself
Yet is certain as meaning . . .

The boots of the men clump
On the boards of the bridge.
The first white wall of the village
Rises through fruit-trees.

Of what was it I was thinking?

So the meaning escapes.

The first white wall of the village . . .
The fruit-trees. . . .

Depression Before Spring

The cock crows
But no queen rises.

The hair of my blonde
Is dazzling,
As the spittle of cows
Threading the wind.

Ho! Ho!

But ki-ki-ri-ki
Brings no rou-cou,
No rou-cou-cou.

But no queen comes
In slipper green.

Earthy Anecdote

Every time the bucks went clattering
Over Oklahoma,
A firecat bristled in the way.

Wherever they went,
They went clattering,
Until they swerved,
In a swift, circular line,
To the right,
Because of the firecat.

Or until they swerved,
In a swift, circular line,
To the left,
Because of the firecat.

The bucks clattered,
The firecat went leaping,
To the right, to the left,
And
Bristled in the way.

Later, the firecat closed his bright eyes
And slept.

Moment of Light

I feel an apparition,
at my back,
an ebon wrack,
of more than man's condition,
that leans upon me there;
and then in back, one more;
and then, still farther back,
still other men aligned;
and then, toujours plus grands, immensities of night,
who, less and less defined
by light
stretch off in the black:

ancestors from the first days of the world.

Before me, I know more,
one smaller at the first, and then one smaller still,
and more and more, that are my son and then his sons.

They lie buried in dumb sleep,
or bury themselves in the future.

And for the time, just one exists:
I.

Just one exists and I am time,
the whole of time.
I am the whole of light.

My flesh alone, for the moment, lives,
my heart alone gives,
my eyes alone have sight.
I am emblazoned, the others, all, are black.
I am the whole of light!
And those behind and those before
are only routineers of rounding time.
In back, they lie perdu in the black: the breachless grime,
(just one exists and I am time)
of an incalculable ether that burns and stings.
My will alone commands me: I am time!
Behind they passed the point of man,
before they are not embryo—I, only, touch with prime.
And that will last long length of time,
think what you will!

I am between two infinite states
on the mid-line dividing,
between the infinite that waits
and the long-abiding,
at the golden spot, where the mid-line swells
and yields to a supple, quivering, deep
inundation.

What do we count? All is for us that live!
Time, even time, and the day's strength and beam.
My fellows, you that live around me,
are you not surprised to be supreme,
on the tense line, in this expanse
of dual circumstance?
And are you not surprised to be the base?
To know that, without you, the scale of lives

on which the eternal poising turns
would sink upon death's pitty under-place?
And are you not surprised to be the very poles?

Let us make signals in the air and cry aloud.
We must leave a wide noise tolling
in the night;
and in the deep of time,
set the wide wind rolling.

[BY JEAN LE ROY]

Le Monocle de Mon Oncle

I

"Mother of heaven, regina of the clouds,
O sceptre of the sun, crown of the moon,
There is not nothing, no, no, never nothing,
Like the clashed edges of two words that kill."
And so I mocked her in magnificent measure.
Or was it that I mocked myself alone?
I wish that I might be a thinking stone.
The sea of spuming thought foists up again
The radiant bubble that she was. And then
A deep up-pouring from some saltier well
Within me, bursts its watery syllable.

II

A red bird flies across the golden floor.
It is a red bird that seeks out his choir
Among the choirs of wind and wet and wing.
A torrent will fall from him when he finds.
Shall I uncrumple this much-crumpled thing?
I am a man of fortune greeting heirs;
For it has come that thus I greet the spring.
These choirs of welcome choir for me farewell.

No spring can follow past meridian.
Yet you persist with anecdotal bliss
To make believe a starry *connaissance.*

III

Is it for nothing, then, that old Chinese
Sat tittivating by their mountain pools
Or in the Yangste studied out their beards?
I shall not play the flat historic scale.
You know how Utamaro's beauties sought
The end of love in their all-speaking braids.
You know the mountainous coiffures of Bath.
Alas! Have all the barbers lived in vain
That not one curl in nature has survived?
Why, without pity on these studious ghosts,
Do you come dripping in your hair from sleep?

IV

This luscious and impeccable fruit of life
Falls, it appears, of its own weight to earth.
When you were Eve, its acrid juice was sweet,
Untasted, in its heavenly, orchard air—
An apple serves as well as any skull
To be the book in which to read a round,
And is as excellent, in that it is composed
Of what, like skulls, comes rotting back to ground.
But it excels in this that as the fruit
Of love, it is a book too mad to read
Before one merely reads to pass the time.

V

In the high West there burns a furious star.
It is for fiery boys that star was set
And for sweet-smelling virgins close to them.
The measure of the intensity of love
Is measure, also, of the verve of earth.

For me, the firefly's quick, electric stroke
Ticks tediously the time of one more year.
And you? Remember how the crickets came
Out of their mother grass, like little kin
In the pale nights, when your first imagery
Found inklings of your bond to all that dust.

VI

If men at forty will be painting lakes
The ephemeral blues must merge for them in one,
The basic slate, the universal hue.
There is a substance in us that prevails.
But in our amours amorists discern
Such fluctuations that their scrivening
Is breathless to attend each quirky turn.
When amorists grow bald, then amours shrink
Into the compass and curriculum
Of introspective exiles, lecturing.
It is a theme for Hyacinth alone.

VII

The mules that angels ride come slowly down
The blazing passes, from beyond the sun.
Descensions of their tinkling bells arrive.
These muleteers are dainty of their way.
Meantime, centurions guffaw and beat
Their shrilling tankards on the table-boards.
This parable, in sense, amounts to this:
The honey of heaven may or may not come,
But that of earth both comes and goes at once.
Suppose these couriers brought amid their train
A damsel heightened by eternal bloom.

VIII

Like a dull scholar, I behold, in love,
An ancient aspect touching a new mind.
It comes, it blooms, it bears its fruit and dies.

This trivial trope reveals a way of truth.
Our bloom is gone. We are the fruit thereof.
Two golden gourds distended on our vines,
We hang like warty squashes, streaked and rayed,
Into the autumn weather, splashed with frost,
Distorted by hale fatness, turned grotesque.
The laughing sky will see the two of us
Washed into rinds by rotting winter rains.

IX

In verses wild with motion, full of din,
Loudened by cries, by clashes, quick and sure
As the deadly thought of men accomplishing
Their curious fates in war, come, celebrate
The faith of forty, ward of Cupido.
Most venerable heart, the lustiest conceit
Is not too lusty for your broadening.
I quiz all sounds, all thoughts, all everything
For the music and manner of the paladins
To make oblation fit. Where shall I find
Bravura adequate to this great hymn?

X

The fops of fancy in their poems leave
Memorabilia of the mystic spouts,
Spontaneously watering their gritty soils.
I am a yeoman, as such fellows go.
I know no magic trees, no balmy boughs,
No silver-ruddy, gold-vermilion fruits.
But, after all, I know a tree that bears
A semblance to the thing I have in mind.
It stands gigantic, with a certain tip
To which all birds come sometime in their time.
But when they go that tip still tips the tree.

XI

If sex were all, then every trembling hand
Could make us squeak, like dolls, the wished-for words.
But note the unconscionable treachery of fate,
That makes us weep, laugh, grunt and groan, and shout
Doleful heroics, pinching gestures forth
From madness or delight, without regard
To that first, foremost law. Anguishing hour!
Last night, we sat beside a pool of pink,
Clippered with lilies, scudding the bright chromes,
Keen to the point of starlight, while a frog
Boomed from his very belly, odious chords.

XII

A blue pigeon it is, that circles the blue sky,
On side-long wing, around and round and round.
A white pigeon it is, that flutters to the ground,
Grown tired of flight. Like a dark rabbi, I
Observed, when young, the nature of mankind,
In lordly study. Every day, I found
Man proved a gobbet in my mincing world.
Like a rose rabbi, later, I pursued,
And still pursue, the origin and course
Of love, but until now I never knew
That fluttering things have so distinct a shade.

Architecture for the Adoration of Beauty

I

What manner of building shall we build for
    the adoration of beauty?
Let us design this chastel de chasteté,
De pensée . . .

Never cease to deploy the structure . . .
Keep the laborers shouldering plinths . . .
Pass the whole of life earing the clink of the
Chisels of the stone-cutters cutting the stones.

II

In this house, what manner of utterance shall
        there be?
What heavenly dithyramb
And cantilene?
What niggling forms of gargoyle patter?
Of what shall the speech be,
In that splay of marble
And of obedient pillars?

III

And how shall those come vested that come there?
In their ugly reminders?
Or gaudy as tulips?
As they climb the stairs
To the group of Flora Coddling Hecuba?
As they climb the flights
To the closes
Overlooking whole seasons?

IV

Let us build the building of light.
Push up the towers
To the cock-tops.
These are the pointings of our edifice,
Which, like a gorgeous palm,
Shall tuft the commonplace.
These are the window-sill
On which the quiet moonlight lies.

V

How shall we hew the sun,
Split it and make blocks,
To build a ruddy palace?
How carve the violet moon
To set in nicks?
Let us fix portals, East and West,
Abhorring green-blue North and blue-green South.
Our chiefest dome a demoiselle of gold.
Pierce the interior with pouring shafts,
In diverse chambers.
Pierce, too, with buttresses of coral air
And purple timbers,
Various argentines,
Embossings of the sky.

VI

And, finally, set guardians in the grounds,
Gray, grewsome grumblers.
For no one proud, nor stiff,
No solemn one, nor pale,
No chafferer, may come
To sully the begonias, nor vex
With holy or sublime ado
The kremlin of kermess.

VII

Only the lusty and the plenteous
Shall walk
The bronze-filled plazas
And the nut-shell esplanades.

Nuances of a Theme by Williams

It's a strange courage
you give me, ancient star:

Shine alone in the sunrise
toward which you lend no part![1]

I

Shine alone, shine nakedly, shine like bronze,
that reflects neither my face nor any inner part
of my being, shine like fire, that mirrors nothing.

II

Lend no part to any humanity that suffuses
you in its own light.
Be not chimera of morning,
Half-man, half-star.
Be not an intelligence,
Like a widow's bird
Or an old horse.

Anecdote of Canna

Huge are the canna in the dreams of
X, the mighty thought, the mighty man.
They fill the terrace of his capitol.

His thought sleeps not. Yet thought that wakes
In sleep may never meet another thought
Or thing . . . Now day-break comes . . .

---

[1] This epigraph is William Carlos Williams's complete poem, "El Hombre."

X promenades the dewy stones,
Observes the canna with a clinging eye,
Observes and then continues to observe.

The Apostrophe to Vincentine

I

I figured you as nude between
Monotonous earth and dark blue sky.
It made you seem so small and lean
And nameless,
Heavenly Vincentine.

II

I saw you then, as warm as flesh,
Brunette,
But yet not too brunette,
As warm, as clean—
Your dress was green,
Was whited green,
Green Vincentine.

III

Then you came walking,
In a group
Of human others,
Voluble.
Yes: you came walking,
Vincentine
Yes: you came talking.

IV

And what I knew you felt
Came then.
Monotonous earth I saw become
Illimitable spheres of you,
And that white animal, so lean,
Turned Vincentine,
Turned heavenly Vincentine,
And that white animal, so lean,
Turned heavenly, heavenly Vincentine.

Life Is Motion

In Oklahoma,
Bonnie and Josie,
Dressed in calico,
Danced around a stump.
They cried,
"Ohoyaho,
Ohoo" . . .
Celebrating the marriage
Of flesh and air.

Fabliau of Florida

Barque of phosphor
On the palmy beach,

Move outward into heaven,
Into the alabasters
And night blues.

Foam and cloud are one.
Sultry moon-monsters
Are dissolving.

Fill your black hull
With white moonlight.

There will never be an end
To this droning of the surf.

Homunculus et La Belle Etoile

In the sea, Biscayne, there prinks
The young emerald, evening star—
Good light for drunkards, poets, widows,
And ladies soon to be married.

By this light the salty fishes
Arch in the sea like tree-branches,
Going in many directions
Up and down.

This light conducts
The thoughts of drunkards, the feelings
Of widows and trembling ladies,
The movements of fishes.

How pleasant an existence it is
That this emerald charms philosophers,
Until they become thoughtlessly willing
To bathe their hearts in later moonlight,

Knowing that they can bring back thought
In the night that is still to be silent,
Reflecting this thing and that,
Before they sleep.

It is better that, as scholars,
They should think hard in the dark cuffs
Of voluminous cloaks,
And shave their heads and bodies.

It might well be that their mistress
Is no gaunt fugitive phantom.
She might, after all, be a wanton,
Abundantly beautiful, eager.

Fecund,
From whose being by starlight, on sea-coast,
The innermost good of their seeking
Might come in the simplest of speech.

It is a good light, then, for those
That know the ultimate Plato,
Tranquillizing with this jewel
The torments of confusion.

The Weeping Burgher

It is with a strange malice
That I distort the world.

Ah! that ill humors
Should mask as white girls.
And ah! that Scaramouche
Should have a black barouche.

The sorry verities!
Yet in excess, continual,
There is cure of sorrow.

Permit that if as ghost I come
Among the people burning in me still,
I come as belle design
Of foppish line.

And I, then, tortured for old speech—
A white of wildly woven rings;
I, weeping in a calcined heart—
My hands such sharp, imagined things.

Peter Parasol

*Aux taureaux Dieu cornes donne
Et sabots durs aux chevaux . . . .*[1]

Why are not women fair,
All, as Andromache—
Having, each one, most praisable
Ears, eyes, soul, skin, hair?

Good God! That all beasts should have
The tusks of the elephant,
Or be beautiful
As large, ferocious tigers are.

It is not so with women.
I wish they were all fair,
And walked in fine clothes,
With parasols, in the afternoon air.

---

[1] "God gives horns to bulls
And hard hooves to horses. . . ."

Exposition of the Contents of a Cab

Victoria Clementina, negress,
Took seven white dogs
To ride in a cab.

Bells of the dogs chinked.
Harness of the horses shuffled
Like brazen shells.

Oh-hé-hé! Fragrant puppets
By the green lake-pallors,
She too is flesh,

And a breech-cloth might wear,
Netted of topaz and ruby
And savage blooms;

Thridding the squawkiest jungle
In a golden sedan,
White dogs at bay.

What breech-cloth might you wear—
Except linen, embroidered
By elderly women?

Ploughing on Sunday

The white cock's tail
Tosses in the wind.
The turkey-cock's tail
Glitters in the sun.

Water in the fields.
The wind pours down.
The feathers flare
And bluster in the wind.

Remus, blow your horn!
I'm ploughing on Sunday,
Ploughing North America.
Blow your horn!

Tum-ti-tum,
Ti-tum-tum-tum!
The turkey-cock's tail
Spreads to the sun.

The white cock's tail
Streams to the moon.
Water in the fields.
The wind pours down.

Banal Sojourn

Two wooden tubs of blue hydrangeas stand at the foot of
   the stone steps.
The sky is a blue gum streaked with rose. The trees are
   black.
The grackles crack their throats of bone in the smooth air.
Moisture and heat have swollen the garden into a slum of
   bloom.
Pardie! Summer is like a fat beast, sleepy in mildew,
Our old bane, green and bloated, serene, who cries,
"That bliss of stars, that princox of evening heaven!"
   reminding of seasons,
When radiance came running down, slim through the
   bareness.
And so it is one damns that green shade at the bottom of
   the land.
   For who can care at the wigs despoiling the Satan ear?
   And who does not seek the sky unfuzzed, soaring to the
      princox?
One has a malady, here, a malady. One feels a malady.

The Indigo Glass in the Grass

Which is real—
This bottle of indigo glass in the grass,
Or the bench with the pot of geraniums, the stained mattress
    and the washed overalls drying in the sun?
Which of these truly contains the world?

Neither one, nor the two together.

Anecdote of the Jar

I placed a jar in Tennessee,
And round it was, upon a hill.
It made the slovenly wilderness
Surround that hill.

The wilderness rose up to it,
And sprawled around, no longer wild.
The jar was round upon the ground
And tall and of a port in air.

It took dominion everywhere.
The jar was gray and bare.
It did not give of bird or bush,
Like nothing else in Tennessee.

Of the Surface of Things

I

In my room, the world is beyond my understanding;
But when I walk I see that it consists of three or four hills and
    a cloud.

II

From my balcony, I survey the yellow air,
Reading where I have written,
"The spring is like a belle undressing."

III

The gold tree is blue.
The singer has pulled his cloak over his head.
The moon is in the folds of the cloak.

The Curtains in the House of the Metaphysician

It comes about that the drifting of these curtains
Is full of long motions; as the ponderous
Deflations of distance; or as clouds
Inseparable from their afternoons;
Or the changing of light, the dropping
Of the silence, wide sleep and solitude
Of night, in which all motion
Is beyond us, as the firmament,
Up-rising and down-falling, bares
The last largeness, bold to see.

The Place of the Solitaires

Let the place of the solitaires
Be a place of perpetual undulation.

Whether it be in mid-sea
On the dark, green water-wheel,
Or on the beaches,
There must be no cessation

Of motion, or of the noise of motion,
The renewal of noise
And manifold continuation;

And, most of the motion of thought
And its restless iteration,

In the place of the solitaires,
Which is to be a place of perpetual undulation.

The Paltry Nude Starts on a Spring Voyage

But not on a shell, she starts,
Archaic, for the sea.
But on the first-found weed
She scuds the glitters,
Noiselessly, like one more wave.

She too is discontent
And would have purple stuff upon her arms,
Tired of the salty harbors,
Eager for the brine and bellowing
Of the high interiors of the sea.

The wind speeds her,
Blowing upon her hands
And watery back.
She touches the clouds, where she goes,
In the circle of her traverse of the sea.

Yet this is meagre play
In the scurry and water-shine,
As her heels foam—
Not as when the goldener nude
Of a later day

Will go, like the centre of sea-green pomp,
In an intenser calm,
Scullion of fate,
Across the spick torrent, ceaselessly,
Upon her irretrievable way.

Colloquy with a Polish Aunt

*Elle savait toutes les légendes du Paradis et tous les contes
de la Pologne.*[1]   *"Revue des Deux Mondes"*

She
How is it that my saints from Voragine,
In their embroidered slippers, touch your spleen?

He
Old pantaloons, duenna of the spring!

She
Imagination is the will of things. . . .
Thus, on the basis of the common drudge,
You dream of women, swathed in indigo,
Holding their books toward the nearer stars,
To read, in secret, burning secrecies. . . .

Invective Against Swans

The soul, O ganders, flies beyond the parks
And far beyond the discords of the wind.

A bronze rain from the sun descending marks
The death of summer, which that time endures

---

[1] "She knew all the legends of Paradise and all the stories of Poland."

Like one who scrawls a listless testament
Of golden quirks and Paphian caricatures,

Bequeathing your white feathers to the moon
And giving your bland motions to the air.

Behold, already on the long parades
The crows anoint the statues with their dirt.

And the soul, O ganders, being lonely, flies
Beyond your chilly chariots, to the skies.

Infanta Marina

Her terrace was the sand
And the palms and the twilight.

She made of the motions of her wrist
The grandiose gestures
Of her thought.

The rumpling of the plumes
Of this creature of the evening
Came to be sleights of sails
Over the sea.

And thus she roamed
In the roamings of her fan,

Partaking of the sea,
And of the evening,
As they flowed around
And utter their subsiding sound.

Cortège for Rosenbloom

Now, the wry Rosenbloom is dead
And his finical carriers tread,
On a hundred legs, the tread
Of the dead.
Rosenbloom is dead.

They carry the wizened one
Of the color of horn
To the sullen hill,
Treading a tread
In unison for the dead.

Rosenbloom is dead.
The tread of the carriers does not halt
On the hill, but turns
Up the sky.
They are bearing his body into the sky.

It is the infants of misanthropes
And the infants of nothingness
That tread
The wooden ascents
Of the ascending of the dead.

It is turbans they wear
And boots of fur
As they tread the boards
In a region of frost,
Viewing the frost.

To a chirr of gongs
And a chitter of cries
And the heavy thrum
Of the endless tread
That they tread.

To a jabber of doom
And a jumble of words
Of the intense poem
Of the strictest prose
Of Rosenbloom.

And they bury him there,
Body and soul,
In a place in the sky.
The lamentable tread!
Rosenbloom is dead.

The Man Whose Pharynx Was Bad

The time of year has grown indifferent.
Mildew of summer and the deepening snow
Are both alike in the routine I know.
I am too dumbly in my being pent.

The wind attendant on the solstices
Blows on the shutters of the metropoles,
Stirring no poet in his sleep, and tolls
The grand ideas of the villages.

The malady of the quotidian . . .
Perhaps, if summer ever came to rest
And lengthened, deepened, comforted, caressed
Through days like oceans in obsidian

Horizons full of night's midsummer blaze;
Perhaps, if winter once could penetrate
Through all its purples to the final slate,
Persisting bleakly in an icy haze;

One might in turn become less diffident—
Out of such mildew plucking neater mould
And spouting new orations of the cold.
One might. One might. But time will not relent.

Palace of the Babies

The disbeliever walked the moonlit place,
Outside of gates of hammered serafin,
Observing the moon-blotches on the walls.

The yellow rocked across the still façades,
Or else sat spinning on the pinnacles,
While he imagined humming sounds and sleep.

The walker in the moonlight walked alone,
And each black window of the building balked
His loneliness and what was in his mind:

If in a shimmering room the babies came,
Drawn close by dreams of fledgling wing,
It was because night nursed them in its fold.

Night nursed not him in whose dark mind
The clambering wings of birds of black revolved,
Making harsh torment of the solitude.

The walker in the moonlight walked alone,
And in his heart his disbelief lay cold.
His broad-brimmed hat came close upon his eyes.

From the Misery of Don Joost

I have finished my combat with the sun;
And my body, the old animal,
Knows nothing more.

The powerful seasons bred and killed,
And were themselves the genii
Of their own ends.

Oh, but the very self of the storm
Of sun and slaves, breeding and death,
The old animal—

The senses and feeling, the very sound
And sight, and all there was of the storm—
Knows nothing more.

The Doctor of Geneva

The doctor of Geneva stamped the sand
That lay impounding the Pacific swell,
Patted his stove-pipe hat and tugged his shawl.

Lacustrine man had never been assailed
By such long-rolling opulent cataracts,
Unless Racine or Bossuet held the like.

He did not quail. A man so used to plumb
The multifarious heavens felt no awe
Before these visible, voluble delugings,

Which yet found means to set his simmering mind
Spinning and hissing with oracular
Notations of the wild, the ruinous waste,

Until the steeples of his city clanked and sprang
In an unburgherly apocalypse.
The doctor used his handkerchief and sighed.

Gubbinal

That strange flower, the sun,
Is just what you say.
Have it your way.

The world is ugly,
And the people are sad.

That tuft of jungle feathers,
That animal eye,
Is just what you say.

That savage of fire,
That seed—
Have it your way.

The world is ugly,
And the people are sad.

The Snow Man

One must have a mind of winter
To regard the frost and the boughs
Of the pine-trees crusted with snow;

And have been cold a long time
To behold the junipers shagged with ice,
The spruces rough in the distant glitter

Of the January sun; and not to think
Of any misery in the sound of the wind,
In the sound of a few leaves,

Which is the sound of the land
Full of the same wind
That is blowing in the same bare place

For the listener, who listens in the snow,
And, nothing himself, beholds
Nothing that is not there and the nothing that is.

Tea at the Palaz of Hoon

Not less because in purple I descended
The western day through what you called
The loneliest air, not less was I myself.

What was the ointment sprinkled on my beard?
What were the hymns that buzzed beside my ears?
What was the sea whose tide swept through me there?

Out of my mind the golden ointment rained,
And my ears made the blowing hymns they heard.
I was myself the compass of that sea:

I was the world in which I walked, and what I saw
Or heard or felt came not but from myself;
And there I found myself more truly and more strange.

The Cuban Doctor

I went to Egypt to escape
The Indian, but the Indian struck
Out of his cloud and from his sky.

This was no worm bred in the moon,
Wriggling far down the phantom air,
And on a comfortable sofa dreamed.

The Indian struck and disappeared.
I knew my enemy was near—I,
Drowsing in summer's sleepiest horn.

Another Weeping Woman

Pour the unhappiness out
From your too bitter heart,
Which grieving will not sweeten.

Poison grows in this dark.
It is in the water of tears
Its black blooms rise.

The magnificent cause of being—
The imagination, the one reality
In this imagined world—

Leaves you
With him for whom no phantasy moves,
And you are pierced by a death.

Of the Manner of Addressing Clouds

Gloomy grammarians in golden gowns,
Meekly you keep the mortal rendezvous,
Eliciting the still sustaining pomps
Of speech which are like music so profound
They seem an exaltation without sound.
Funest philosophers and ponderers,
Their evocations are the speech of clouds.
So speech of your processionals returns
In the casual evocations of your tread
Across the stale, mysterious seasons. These
Are the music of meet resignation; these
The responsive, still sustaining pomps for you
To magnify, if in that drifting waste
You are to be accompanied by more
Than mute bare splendors of the sun and moon.

Of Heaven Considered as a Tomb

What word have you, interpreters, of men
Who in the tomb of heaven walk by night,
The darkened ghosts of our old comedy?
Do they believe they range the gusty cold,
With lanterns borne aloft to light the way,
Freemen of death, about and still about
To find whatever it is they seek? Or does
That burial, pillared up each day as porte
And spiritous passage into nothingness,
Foretell each night the one abysmal night,
When the host shall no more wander, nor the light
Of the steadfast lanterns creep across the dark?
Make hue among the dark comedians,
Halloo them in the topmost distances
For answer from their icy Elysée.

The Load of Sugar-Cane

The going of the glade-boat
Is like water flowing;

Like water flowing
Through the green saw-grass,
Under the rainbows;

Under the rainbows
That are like birds,
Turning, bedizened,

While the wind still whistles
As kildeer do,

When they rise
At the red turban
Of the boatman.

Hibiscus on the Sleeping Shores

I say now, Fernando, that on that day
The mind roamed as a moth roams,
Among the blooms beyond the open sand;

And that whatever noise the motion of the waves
Made on the sea-weeds and the covered stones
Disturbed not even the most idle ear.

Then it was that that monstered moth
Which had lain folded against the blue
And the colored purple of the lazy sea,

And which had drowsed along the bony shores,
Shut to the blather that the water made,
Rose up besprent and sought the flaming red

Dabbled with yellow pollen—red as red
As the flag above the old café—
And roamed there all the stupid afternoon.

The Bird with the Coppery, Keen Claws

Above the forest of the parakeets,
A parakeet of parakeets prevails,
A pip of life amid a mort of tails.

(The rudiments of tropics are around,
Aloe of ivory, pear of rusty rind).
His lids are white because his eyes are blind.

He is not paradise of parakeets,
Of his gold ether, golden alguazil,
Except because he broods there and is still.

Panache upon panache, his tails deploy
Upward and outward, in green-vented forms,
His tip a drop of water full of storms.

But though the turbulent tinges undulate
As his pure intellect applies its laws,
He moves not on his coppery, keen claws.

He munches a dry shell while he exerts
His will, yet never ceases, perfect cock,
To flare, in the sun-pallor of his rock.

Lulu Gay

Lulu sang of barbarians before the eunuchs
Of gobs, who called her orchidean,
Sniffed her and slapped heavy hands
Upon her.
She made the eunuchs ululate.
She described for them
The manners of the barbarians
What they did with their thumbs.
The eunuchs heard her
With continual ululation.
She described how the barbarians kissed her
With their wide mouths
And breaths as true
As the gum of the gum-tree.
"Olu" the eunuchs cried. "Ululalu."

Lulu Morose

Is there a sharp edge?
Is there a sharp edge?
On which to lean
Like a belly puckered by a spear.

The cliffs are rough.
Are rough
And not all birds sing cuck
Sing coo, sing cuck, cuckoo.

Oh! Sal, the butcher's wife ate clams
And died amid uproarious damns.
And mother nature sick of silk
Shot lightning at the kind cow's milk.

And father nature, full of butter
Made the maelstrom oceans mutter.
Stabbing at his teat-like corns
From an ottoman of thorns.

Hymn from a Watermelon Pavilion

You dweller in the dark cabin,
To whom the watermelon is always purple,
Whose garden is wind and moon,

Of the two dreams, night and day,
What lover, what dreamer, would choose
The one obscured by sleep?

Here is the plantain by your door
And the best cock of red feather
That crew before the clocks.

A feme may come, leaf-green,
Whose coming may give revel
Beyond revelries of sleep,

Yes, and the blackbird spread its tail,
So that the sun may speckle,
While it creaks hail.
You dweller in the dark cabin,
Rise, since rising will not waken,
And hail, cry hail, cry hail.

Stars at Tallapoosa

The lines are straight and swift between the stars.
The night is not the cradle that they cry,
The criers, undulating the deep-oceaned phrase.
The lines are much too dark and much too sharp.

The mind herein attains simplicity.
There is no moon, no single, silvered leaf.
The body is no body to be seen
But is an eye that studies its black lid.

Let these be your delight, secretive hunter,
Wading the sea-lines, moist and ever-mingling,
Mounting the earth-lines, long and lax, lethargic.
These lines are swift and fall without diverging.

The melon-flower nor dew nor web of either
Is like to these. But in yourself is like:
A sheaf of brilliant arrows flying straight,
Flying and falling straightway for their pleasure,

Their pleasure that is all bright-edged and cold;
Or, if not arrows, then the nimblest motions,
Making recoveries of young nakedness
And the lost vehemence the midnights hold.

Bantams in Pine-Woods

Chieftain Iffucan of Azcan in caftan
Of tan with henna hackles, halt!

Damned universal cock, as if the sun
Was blackamoor to bear your blazing tail.

Fat! Fat! Fat! Fat! I am the personal.
Your world is you. I am my world.

You ten-foot poet among inchlings. Fat!
Begone! An inchling bristles in these pines,

Bristles, and points their Appalachian tangs,
And fears not portly Azcan nor his hoos.

The Ordinary Women

Then from their poverty they rose,
From dry catarrhs, and to guitars
They flitted
Through the palace walls.

They flung monotony behind,
Turned from their want, and, nonchalant,
They crowded
The nocturnal halls.

The lacquered loges huddled there
Mumbled zay-zay and a-zay, a-zay.
The moonlight
Fubbed the girandoles.

And the cold dresses that they wore,
In the vapid haze of the window-bays,
Were tranquil
As they leaned and looked

From the window-sills at the alphabets,
At beta b and gamma g,
To study
The canting curlicues

Of heaven and of the heavenly script.
And there they read of marriage-bed.
Ti-lill-o!
And they read right long.

The gaunt guitarists on the strings
Rumbled a-day and a-day, a-day.
The moonlight
Rose on the beachy floors.

How explicit the coiffures became,
The diamond point, the sapphire point,
The sequins
Of the civil fans!

Insinuations of desire,
Puissant speech, alike in each,
Cried quittance
To the wickless halls.

Then from their poverty they rose,
From dry guitars, and to catarrhs
They flitted
Through the palace walls.

Frogs Eat Butterflies. Snakes Eat Frogs.
Hogs Eat Snakes. Men Eat Hogs

It is true that the rivers went nosing like swine,
Tugging at banks, until they seemed
Bland belly-sounds in somnolent troughs,

That the air was heavy with the breath of these swine,
The breath of turgid summer, and
Heavy with thunder's rattapallax,

That the man who erected this cabin, planted
This field, and tended it awhile,
Knew not the quirks of imagery,

That the hours of his indolent, arid days,
Grotesque with this nosing in banks,
This somnolence and rattapallax,

Seemed to suckle themselves on his arid being,
As the swine-like rivers suckled themselves
While they went seaward to the sea-mouths.

A High-Toned Old Christian Woman

Poetry is the supreme fiction, madame.
Take the moral law and make a nave of it
And from the nave build haunted heaven. Thus,
The conscience is converted into palms,
Like windy citherns hankering for hymns.
We agree in principle. That's clear. But take
The opposing law and make a peristyle,
And from the peristyle project a masque
Beyond the planets. Thus, our bawdiness,
Unpurged by epitaph, indulged at last,
Is equally converted into palms,
Squiggling like saxophones. And palm for palm,
Madame, we are where we began. Allow,
Therefore, that in the planetary scene
Your disaffected flagellants, well-stuffed,
Smacking their muzzy bellies in parade,
Proud of such novelties of the sublime,
Such tink and tank and tunk-a-tunk-tunk,
May, merely may, madame, whip from themselves
A jovial hullabaloo among the spheres.
This will make widows wince. But fictive things
Wink as they will. Wink most when widows wince.

O, Florida, Venereal Soil

A few things for themselves,
Convolvulus and coral,
Buzzards and live-moss,
Tiestas from the keys,
A few things for themselves,
Florida, venereal soil,
Disclose to the lover.

The dreadful sundry of this world,
The Cuban, Polodowsky,
The Mexican women,
The negro undertaker
Killing the time between corpses
Fishing for crawfish . . .
Virgin of boorish births,

Swiftly in the nights,
In the porches of Key West,
Behind the bougainvilleas,
After the guitar is asleep,
Lasciviously as the wind,
You come tormenting,
Insatiable,

When you might sit,
A scholar of darkness,
Sequestered over the sea,
Wearing a clear tiara
Of red and blue and red,
Sparkling, solitary, still,
In the high sea-shadow.

Donna, donna, dark,
Stooping in indigo gown
And cloudy constellations,
Conceal yourself or disclose
Fewest things to the lover—
A hand that bears a thick-leaved fruit,
A pungent bloom against your shade.

The Emperor of Ice-Cream

Call the roller of big cigars,
The muscular one, and bid him whip
In kitchen cups concupiscent curds.
Let the wenches dawdle in such dress
As they are used to wear, and let the boys
Bring flowers in last month's newspapers.
Let be be finale of seem.
The only emperor is the emperor of ice-cream.

Take from the dresser of deal,
Lacking the three glass knobs, that sheet
On which she embroidered fantails once
And spread it so as to cover her face.
If her horny feet protrude, they come
To show how cold she is, and dumb.
Let the lamp affix its beam.
The only emperor is the emperor of ice-cream.

To the One of Fictive Music

Sister and mother and diviner love,
And of the sisterhood of the living dead
Most near, most clear, and of the clearest bloom,
And of the fragrant mothers the most dear

And queen, and of diviner love the day
And flame and summer and sweet fire, no thread
Of cloudy silver sprinkles in your gown
Its venom of renown, and on your head
No crown is simpler than the simple hair.

Now, of the music summoned by the birth
That separates us from the wind and sea,
Yet leaves them in us until earth becomes,
By being so much of the things we are,
Gross effigy and simulacrum, none
Gives motion to perfection more serene
Than yours, out of our imperfections wrought,
Most rare, or ever of more kindred air
In the laborious weaving that you wear.

For so retentive of themselves are men
That music is intensest which proclaims
The near, the clear, and vaunts the clearest bloom,
And of all vigils musing the obscure
That apprehends the most which sees and names,
As in your name, an image that is sure,
Among the arrant spices of the sun,
O bough and bush and scented vine, in whom
We give ourselves our likest issuance.

Yet not too like, yet not so like to be
Too near, too clear, saving a little to endow
Our feigning with the strange unlike, whence springs
The difference that heavenly pity brings.
For this, musician, in your girdle-fixed
Bear other perfumes. On your pale head wear
A band entwining, set with fatal stones.
Unreal, give back to us what once you gave:
The imagination that we spurned and crave.

Alphabetical List of Titles

page

Anecdote of Canna	47
Anecdote of Men by the Thousand	35
Anecdote of the Jar	55
Another Weeping Woman	66
Apostrophe to Vincentine, The	48
Architecture for the Adoration of Beauty	44
Banal Sojourn	54
Bantams in Pine-Woods	72
Bird with the Coppery, Keen Claws, The	69
Bowl	18
Carnet de Voyage	1
Colloquy with a Polish Aunt	58
Cortège for Rosenbloom	60
Cuban Doctor, The	66
Curtains in the House of the Metaphysician, The	56
Cy Est Pourtraicte, Madame Ste Ursule, et Les Unze Mille Vierges	6
Depression Before Spring	37
Disillusionment of Ten O'Clock	10
Doctor of Geneva, The	63
Domination of Black	13
Earthy Anecdote	37
Emperor of Ice-Cream, The	77
Explanation	27
Exposition of the Contents of a Cab	53
Fabliau of Florida	49

Florist Wears Knee-Breeches, The	15
Frogs Eat Butterflies. Snakes Eat Frogs. Hogs Eat Snakes Men Eat Hogs	74
From a Junk	4
From the Misery of Don Joost	63
Gray Room	26
Gubbinal	64
Hibiscus on the Sleeping Shores	68
High-Toned Old Christian Woman, A	75
Home Again	4
Homunculus et La Belle Etoile	50
Hymn from a Watermelon Pavilion	71
Indigo Glass in the Grass, The	55
Infanta Marina	59
Inscription for a Monument	18
Invective Against Swans	58
Le Monocle de Mon Oncle	40
"Lettres d'un Soldat"	29
Life Is Motion	49
Load of Sugar-Cane, The	68
Lulu Gay	70
Lulu Morose	70
Man Whose Pharynx Was Bad, The	61
Meditation	26
Metaphors of a Magnifico	36
Moment of Light	38
Nuances of a Theme by Williams	47
O, Florida, Venereal Soil	76
Of Heaven Considered as a Tomb	67
Of the Manner of Addressing Clouds	67
Of the Surface of Things	55
Ordinary Women, The	73
Palace of the Babies	62
Paltry Nude Starts on a Spring Voyage, The	57
Peter Parasol	52

Peter Quince at the Clavier   7
Phases   4
Place of the Solitaires, The   56
Plot Against the Giant, The   28
Ploughing on Sunday   53
Primordia   19
Silver Plough-Boy, The   10
Six Significant Landscapes   16
Snow Man, The   64
Song   15
Stars at Tallapoosa   72
Sunday Morning   11
Tattoo   144
Tea   6
Tea at the Palaz of Hoon   65
Theory   27
Thirteen Ways of Looking at a Blackbird   23
To the One of Fictive Music   77
To the Roaring Wind   22
Valley Candle   22
Weeping Burgher, The   51
Wind Shifts, The   25
Worms at Heaven's Gate, The   19

Alphabetical List of First Lines

	page
A black figure dances in a black field	10
A few things for themselves	76
A great fish plunges in the dark	4
Above the forest of the parakeets	69
Ach, Mutter	27
All over Minnesota	19
Although you sit in a room that is gray	26
Among twenty snowy mountains	23
An odor from a star	1
An old man sits	16
At night, by the fire	13
Back within the valley	4
Barque of phosphor	49
But not on a shell, she starts	57
Call the roller of big cigars	77
Chieftain Iffucan of Azcan in caftan	72
Complacencies of the peignoir, and late	11
Every time the bucks went clattering	37
For what emperor	18
Gloomy grammarians in golden gowns	67
Her terrace was the sand	59
How is that my saints from Voragine	58
How long have I meditated, O Prince	26
Huge are the canna in the dreams of	47
I am what is around me	27
I feel an apparition	38

I figured you as nude between   48
I have finished my combat with the sun   63
I placed a jar in Tennessee   55
I say now, Fernando, that on that day   68
I went to Egypt to escape   66
In my room, the world is beyond my understanding   55
In Oklahoma   49
In the sea, Biscayne, there prinks   50
Is there a sharp edge?   70
It comes about that the drifting of these curtains   56
It is true that the rivers went nosing like swine   74
It is with a strange malice   51
Just as my fingers on these keys   7
Let the place of the solitaires   56
Lulu sang of barbarians before the eunuchs   70
Mother of heaven, regina of the clouds   40
My candle burned alone in an immense valley   22
My flowers are reflected   15
Not less because in purple I descended   65
Now, the wry Rosenbloom is dead   60
One must have a mind of winter   64
Out of the tomb, we bring Badroulbadour   19
Poetry is the supreme fiction, madame   75
Pour the unhappiness out   66
Shine alone, shine nakedly, shine like bronze   47
Sister and mother and diviner love   77
That strange flower, the sun   64
The cock crows   37
The disbeliever walked the moonlit place   62
The doctor of Geneva stamped the sand   63
The going of the glade-boat   68
The houses are haunted   10
The light is like a spider   14
The lines are straight and swift between the stars   72
The soul, he said, is composed   35

The soul, O ganders, flies beyond the parks   58
The spirit wakes in the night wind—is naked   29
The time of year has grown indifferent   61
The white cock's tail   53
Then from their poverty they rose   73
There are great things doing   15
There's a little square in Paris   4
This is how the wind shifts   25
To the imagined lives   18
Twenty men crossing a bridge   36
Two wooden tubs of blue hydrangeas stand at
     the foot of the stone steps   54
Ursula, in a garden, found   6
Victoria Clementina, negress   53
What manner of building shall we build for
     the adoration of beauty?   44
What syllable are you seeking   22
What word have you, interpreters, of men   67
When the elephant's-ear in the park   6
When this yokel comes maundering   28
Which is real—   55
Why are not women fair   52
You dweller in the dark cabin   71